W9-CKI-642

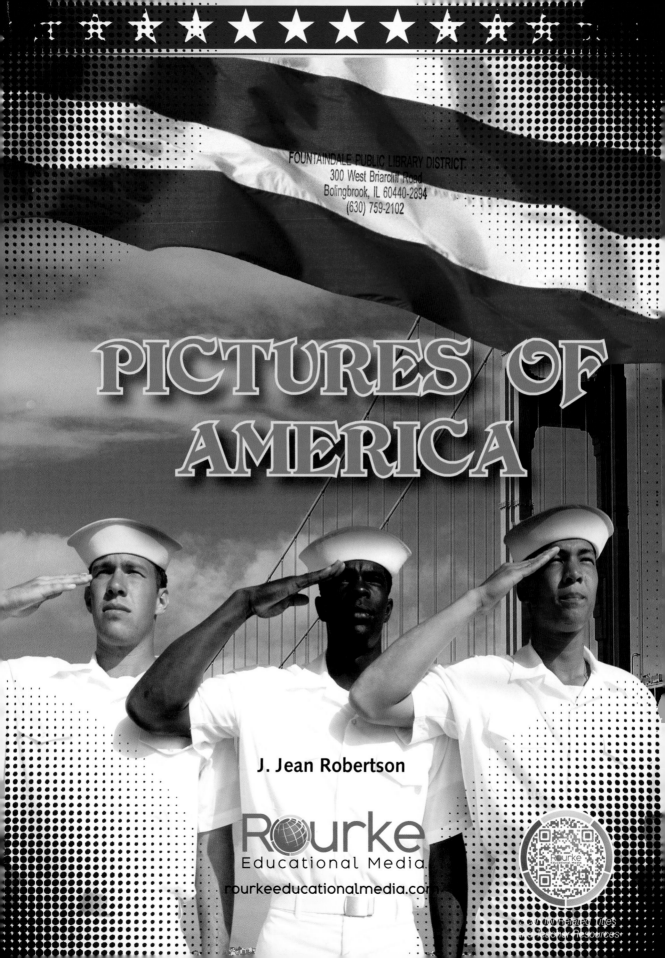

PICTURES OF AMERICA

J. Jean Robertson

Rourke
Educational Media.

rourkeeducationalmedia.com

Before Reading:

Building Academic Vocabulary and Background Knowledge

Before reading a book, it is important to tap into what your child or students already know about the topic. This will help them develop their vocabulary, increase their reading comprehension, and make connections across the curriculum.

1. *Look at the cover of the book. What will this book be about?*
2. *What do you already know about the topic?*
3. *Let's study the Table of Contents. What will you learn about in the book's chapters?*
4. *What would you like to learn about this topic? Do you think you might learn about it from this book? Why or why not?*
5. *Use a reading journal to write about your knowledge of this topic. Record what you already know about the topic and what you hope to learn about the topic.*
6. *Read the book.*
7. *In your reading journal, record what you learned about the topic and your response to the book.*
8. *After reading the book complete the activities below.*

Content Area Vocabulary
Read the list. What do these words mean?

admirably
campaign
emblems
icons
image
magnet
script
symbol
synonymous
turbulent

After Reading:

Comprehension and Extension Activity

After reading the book, work on the following questions with your child or students in order to check their level of reading comprehension and content mastery.

1. *What things represent America for you? (Text to self connection)*
2. *What started the education of safety in nature? (Summarize)*
3. *How did American business contribute to the American symbols? (Asking questions)*
4. *What does Route 66 symbolize? (Summarize)*
5. *Where do you see government symbols? (Asking questions)*

Extension Activity

You read about many cities, people, and businesses that symbolize America. Are there any new symbols today that will stand throughout history and represent America? What symbolizes America for you? Create a new design for the dollar bill using symbols that represent America. Write a description for your design explaining why you chose to use the symbols you did.

TABLE OF CONTENTS

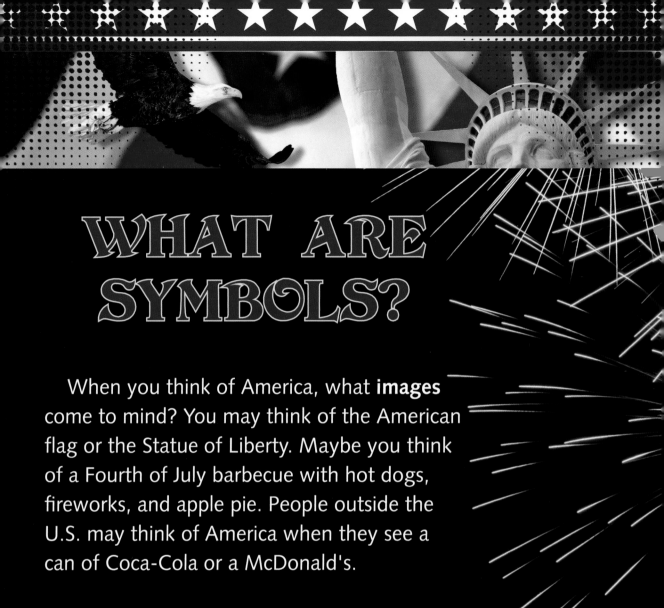

WHAT ARE SYMBOLS?

When you think of America, what **images** come to mind? You may think of the American flag or the Statue of Liberty. Maybe you think of a Fourth of July barbecue with hot dogs, fireworks, and apple pie. People outside the U.S. may think of America when they see a can of Coca-Cola or a McDonald's.

Sometimes, pictures and **symbols** have a greater meaning than what you see. There is a saying, "A picture is worth a thousand words." Think of all the pictures that come to mind when you think about the United States of America. What do these pictures mean to you?

PATRIOTIC SYMBOLS

During the war of 1812, Sam Wilson supplied barrels of meat, labeled "U.S." to the army. Although the label was meant to stand for United States, one of Wilson's workers guessed that the "U.S." stood for Uncle Sam. It made sense to people. The name Uncle Sam became **synonymous** with the United States.

This Uncle Sam statue was erected by the town of Arlington, Massachusetts in honor of Samuel Wilson, who was born in Arlington.

Another war, World War I, came in 1914. Uncle Sam came back in perhaps the most famous poster in the world. Millions of copies have been printed. You have probably seen this poster that was created by James Montgomery Flagg. It read, "I want you for the U.S. Army."

When the United States went to war again, World War II, the Uncle Sam poster reappeared. It was used to encourage patriotism.

The image has changed a bit over time, but all the images are recognizable as Uncle Sam.

Other posters helped encourage the war effort at home. During World War II, there was an increased need for factory workers. But because of the war, there were fewer men available to do the work. In the early 1940s, most women did not work away from home. Those who were employed usually did office work. Women were encouraged to fill the vacant factory positions, and did so **admirably**.

The "We Can Do It!" poster was produced by J. Howard Miller to encourage the female workers. Redd Evans and John Jacob Loeb wrote a popular song called "Rosie the Riveter." In 1943, Norman Rockwell created a painting called "Rosie the Riveter," which appeared on the cover of *The Saturday Evening Post.*

Today, the best-known **image** is the "We Can Do It!" poster. It has come to represent women's ability to be successful in the workplace.

J. Howard Miller created this "We Can Do It!" poster for the Westinghouse Company in 1942.

Other popular posters help educate Americans about safety. The U.S. Forest Service started a **campaign** to prevent forest fires. The Smokey Bear campaign began in 1944 with an imaginary bear and the phrase, "Smokey Says—Care Will Prevent 9 out of 10 Forest Fires."

The campaign took off. Soon after, a burned bear cub was rescued from a forest fire in 1950. America fell in love with him. He received fan mail from both children and adults. Many people were interested in his recovery.

ONLY YOU CAN PREVENT FOREST FIRES!

The Smokey Bear campaign has helped educate generations of Americans about wildfires.

When the rescued little bear cub was healed from his burns, it was decided that he was the perfect bear to remind Americans to be careful with outdoor fires. The Smokey Bear cub was moved to the National Zoo in Washington, D.C.

Smokey Bear is still used to educate people about fire safety. Today, his slogan is, "Only You Can Prevent Wildfires."

Smokey Bear had millions of visitors at his home in the National Zoo.

GEOGRAPHIC SYMBOLS

The largest and most well-known city of the United States is New York City. Sometimes called "the Big Apple," New York City is known as the city that never sleeps. Much of the night activity can be found at Times Square. Times Square is the home of the theater district. As such, it is a **magnet** for residents and visitors alike. In fact, it is one of the most visited places in the world.

Many people visit Times Square just to see the billboards. Because they are such a tourist attraction, zoning in Times Square requires buildings to be covered with billboards.

Every New Year's Eve, people all over the world watch the ball drop at midnight in Times Square.

Freedom Fact!

More than 39 million people visit Times Square each year.

Through history, many Americans have headed west in order to start new lives. For many, this path was over what is perhaps the United States' most famous highway: Route 66.

This 2,500-mile (4,000-kilometer) road linked Chicago and Los Angeles and was one of the first paved highways in the U.S. In the 1930s, hundreds of thousands of farmers traveled Route 66 to California. Their farms in the Dust Bowl had dried up, and they hoped to find work and new opportunities in California.

The tiny town of Adrian, Texas is halfway between Chicago and Los Angeles on Old Route 66.

Later, when soldiers returning from World War II were looking to start new lives back in the U.S., they too followed Route 66 to California. The highway symbolized optimism and freedom for many Americans.

Many roads now cross the United States. Interstate highways have bypassed Route 66, but its place in history is secure.

United States

Missouri

Illinois

California

Arizona

New Mexico

Texas

Oklahoma

Route 66

The Golden Gate Bridge is considered to be one of the most beautiful bridges in the world.

On the Pacific Coast of the country, the graceful span of the Golden Gate Bridge welcomes the world to San Francisco, California. The Golden Gate Bridge spans 1.7 miles (2.7 kilometers) of **turbulent** water where the Pacific Ocean currents rush through the canyon below the bridge into San Francisco Bay.

Joseph Strauss, the engineer who designed and built the bridge had to consider in his design, not only the swift water current, but the strong winds in the area. Construction of the bridge began in 1933 and was completed in 1937. It held the title of "Longest Suspension Bridge in the World" for almost 30 years.

CORPORATE SYMBOLS

A number of companies are also strongly associated with America. Ford Motor Company, for example, has a well-established place in American history.

Henry Ford (1863–1947)

In 1896, Henry Ford completed his first self-propelled vehicle. He continued experimenting, evaluating, and improving his inventions. He worked with some of his employees to build a better, cheaper car, and in 1908 the Model T was introduced. It was a huge success. By 1922, half of the cars in America were Model Ts.

Ford was not always successful, but he learned from his failures. He was willing to work with others and learn from them. Ford was interested in improving the lives of those around him. He made an important contribution to the transportation industry and American society. His company still operates today, over one hundred years later.

Ford built more than 15 million Model Ts, which sold for as low as $260.

Its red and white **script** is one of the most recognizable logos in the world. And for many people, it doesn't get more American than Coca-Cola.

In 1886, Dr. John S. Pemberton, a pharmacist in Atlanta, Georgia created a tasty syrup, which he mixed with carbonated water. It was a hit. It was sold for 5 cents at a drug store soda fountain. Pemberton's bookkeeper, Frank M. Robinson named the popular new beverage "Coca-Cola."

Dr. John S. Pemberton
(1831–1888)

Pemberton sold off much of Coca-Cola to different businessmen. In 1899, three businessmen from Chattanooga, Tennessee bought the right to sell Coca-Cola in bottles. They chose to develop and trademark the famous contoured bottle, now known as a coke bottle.

Coca-Cola has never lost its popularity. Coca-Cola is now bottled and sold in more than 200 countries around the world.

In the late 1800s, many pharmacies served hand-made soda drinks.

Like Coca-Cola, the Golden Arches of McDonald's restaurants are highly recognizable. It is the world's largest restaurant chain. The restaurant operates in more than 100 countries, with more than 35,000 restaurants serving nearly 70 million people every day.

The original purpose of the Golden Arches was two-fold. A single arch was placed at either end of the building for support. The other purpose of the arches was that it could be easily seen from the street as an advertisement for the hamburger stand.

With its speedy service that catered to both drive-thru and dine-in customers, McDonald's grew in popularity. By introducing Happy Meals and the mascot Ronald McDonald, the restaurant soon became a great family location. In the 1960s, the Golden Arches logo changed to become the two overlapping arches seen today.

McDonald's did not introduce its popular Big Mac hamburger until 1968.

Freedom Fact!

First introduced in 1977, Happy Meals helped make McDonald's a family restaurant.

Walt Disney's Mickey Mouse was first introduced to moviegoers in 1928. Mickey was first seen in black and white silent movies, but by 1935, he appeared in both color and sound. The squeaky-voiced mouse became famous around the world.

With the popular mouse as the symbol, Walt Disney and his brother Roy founded Disney Studios. Roy was the businessman and Walt was the creative genius. Disney's productions moved from short silent movies to feature-length films using animation and live action. The studio released 81 films during Walt Disney's lifetime.

Walt Disney (1901–1966) is recognized as a pioneer in the art of animation.

The company built amusement parks in Florida and California that became popular family vacation spots. Other Disney characters, such as Pluto, Minnie Mouse, Goofy, and Donald Duck greet the park's visitors. But the world-famous Mickey Mouse remains the park's most popular character.

The Walt Disney Company continues to operate its parks and make family-oriented entertainment. It's television network, the Disney Channel, and its animation studio, Pixar, have created some of the most popular entertainment for children and adults.

More than 50 million people visit Walt Disney World each year.

OFFICIAL SYMBOLS

The U.S. government uses some symbols to represent America. These symbols may appear on government documents, buildings, money, and more. Some official symbols, **emblems**, or **icons** of the United States of America include:

☆ Great Seal of the United States

☆ Oak tree

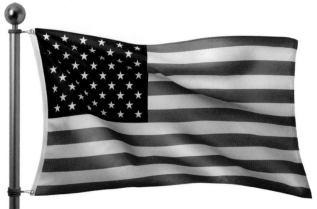

☆ United States Flag

☆ Red rose in full bloom

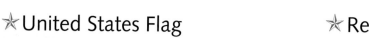

Different things say "The United States of America" to different people. What says "The United States of America" to you?

★American Bald Eagle

★Statue of Liberty

★Liberty Bell

TIMELINE

1776 ——— *Liberty Bell is first rung.*

1777 ——— *United States Flag is adopted.*

1782 ——— *American Bald Eagle is adopted as official bird emblem of the United States.*

1782 ——— *Great Seal of the United States is adopted.*

1812 ——— *Uncle Sam becomes synonymous with the United States.*

1886 ——— *Statue of Liberty is dedicated a national memorial.*

1886 ——— *Coca-Cola is invented.*

1903 ——— *Ford Motor Company is founded.*

1907 —— *New Years Eve ball drop begins in Times Square.*

1926 —— *Popular road from Chicago to California is named Route 66.*

1928 —— *Disney's Mickey Mouse first appears on screen.*

1931 —— *"The Star-Spangled Banner" is approved as the U.S. national anthem.*

1937 —— *Golden Gate Bridge is completed.*

1941 —— *Rosie the Riveter becomes a symbol to promote the war effort.*

1942 —— *Pledge of Allegiance is written.*

1944 —— *Smokey Bear campaign to prevent forest fires begins.*

1953 —— *Golden Arches are introduced to McDonald's restaurant.*

1986 —— *Red rose in full bloom is dedicated as the U.S. national flower.*

2004 —— *Oak tree is designated as the U.S. national tree.*

GLOSSARY

admirably (AD-muh-ruh-blee): in a praiseworthy way

campaign (kam-PAYN): a series of activities designed to create a specific result

emblems (EM-blumz): items used to represent something

icons (EYE-konz): pictures representing something

image (IM-ij): pictures or sculptures

magnet (MAG-nit): something that attracts people

script (SKRIPT): cursive writing

symbols (SIM-buhlz): designs used to represent something

synonymous (si-NON-uh-muss): meaning the same thing

turbulent (TUR-byuh-luhnt): moving roughly and erratically

INDEX

SHOW WHAT YOU KNOW

1. What character has been used to encourage patriotism since 1812?
2. What must be attached to all businesses in Times Square in order to meet the zoning regulations?
3. Why did farmers travel Route 66 to California in the 1930s?
4. How did Ford Motor company effect American history?
5. What is the official bird emblem of the United States?

WEBSITES TO VISIT

www.smokeybear.com/vault/story_main.asp
www.timessquare.com
www.nps.gov/pwro/collection/website/pics.htm

ABOUT THE AUTHOR

J. Jean Robertson, also known as Bushka to her grandchildren and many other kids, lives in San Antonio, Florida with her husband. She is retired after many years of teaching. She loves to read, write books for children, and travel. She has traveled to a number of interesting countries, but is always thankful to be an American citizen.

Meet The Author!
www.meetREMauthors.com

www.rourkeeducationalmedia.com

PHOTO CREDITS: Title page © Visions of America LLC; Top bar © Steve Collender; pag 4 © parema; page 6 © Daderot; page 7 © james Montgomery Flagg/Library of Congress; page 8 © M. Marshall/Wikipedia; page 9 © J. Howard Miller/Museum of American History/Smithsonian Institution; page 13 © stu99; page 14 © Quester Mark, pidjoe; page 16 © compassandcamera; page 18 © Library of Congress; page 20 © Murat Koc, page 21 © LyaCattel; page 22 © Justin Cleary; page 24 © Radu Razvan; apge 25 © Irian Silvestrova; page 37 © Marilyn Barbone, isslee.com
Edited by: Jill Sherman

Cover design by: Nicola Stratford, nicolastratford.com
Interior design by: Renee Brady

Library of Congress PCN Data

Pictures of America / J. Jean Robertson
(Symbols of Freedom)
ISBN 978-1-62717-736-8 (hard cover)
ISBN 978-1-62717-858-7 (soft cover)
ISBN 978-1-62717-969-0 (e-Book)
Library of Congress Control Number: 2014935661

Printed in the United States of America, North Mankato, Minnesota

Also Available as: